First published in Great Britain in 1996 by Brockhampton Press,
a member of the Hodder Headline Group,
20 Bloomsbury Street, London WC1B 3QA.

This series of little gift books was made by Frances Banfield,
Kate Brown, Laurel Clark, Penny Clarke, Clive Collins, Melanie
Cumming, Nick Diggory, Deborah Gill, David Goodman, Douglas
Hall, Maureen Hill, Nick Hutchison, John Hybert, Kate Hybert,
Douglas Ingram, Simon London, Patrick McCreeth, Morse Modaberi,
Tara Neill, Anne Newman, Grant Oliver, Michelle Rogers,
Nigel Soper, Karen Sullivan and Nick Wells.

Compilation and selection copyright
© 1996 Brockhampton Press.

ISBN 1 86019 460 5
A copy of the CIP data is available from the
British Library upon request.

Produced for Brockhampton Press by Flame Tree Publishing,
part of The Foundry Creative Media Company Limited,
The Long House, Antrobus Road, Chiswick W4 5HY.

Printed and bound in Italy by L.E.G.O. Spa.

The Funny Book of
GOLF

Words selected by
Bob Hale

Cartoons by
DICKY HOWETT

BROCKHAMPTON PRESS

Golf sometimes demands physical courage from spectators, witness the occasion when Mr Spiro Agnew (once Vice-President of the United States) aimed to the north and wounded those standing to his east.

I owe a lot to my parents, especially my mother and my father.
Greg Norman

And, on the eve of the Bob Hope Classic ... an interview with the man himself, Gerry Ford.
Jim Rosenthal

Golf is a good walk spoiled.
Mark Twain

I'm a golf widow – any minute now!

Every day I try to tell myself this is going
to be fun today. I try to put myself in a great
frame of mind before I go out - then I
screw it up with the first shot.
Johnny Miller, **Golf Magazine**

Golf is a wonderful exercise. You can stand on your
feet for hours, watching somebody else putt.
Will Rogers

'Mildred, shut up,' cried the golfer at his
nagging wife. 'Shut up or you'll drive me
out of my mind.' 'That,' snapped Mildred,
'wouldn't be a drive. That would be a putt.'
Robert McCune, **The World's Best Golf Jokes**

A laugh a minute is my caddy...

You're not much good are you? You keep missing it...

Golf is like a love affair. If you don't take it too seriously, it's no fun; if you do take it seriously, it breaks your heart.

Arnold Daly

All I've got against it is that it takes you so far from the club house.

Eric Linklater

Give me my golf clubs, fresh air, and a beautiful partner, and you can keep my golf clubs and the fresh air.

Jack Benny

If a ball comes to rest in dangerous proximity
to a hippopotamus or crocodile, another
ball may be dropped at a safe distance,
no nearer the hole, without penalty.

Nyanza Club (British East Africa) rule, 1950

Show me a man who is a good loser, and I'll show
you a man who is playing golf with his boss.

Anonymous

Give me a millionaire with a bad backswing,
and I can have a very pleasant afternoon.

George Law

I'm hitting the woods just great, but I'm
having a terrible time hitting out of them.

Harry Toscano

Why Hector – I see your putt runneth over!

Golf: a game in which you claim the privileges of age, and retain the playthings of childhood.

Samuel Johnson

We beseech you, lord, to heal our slice,
to straighten our hook,
to carve our divots truly,
to improve our lie,
making it just a tad better than our opponents.

Monsignor Richard E. McCabe

Old golfers never die, they just putter away.

Anonymous

The reason the pro tells you to keep your head down is so you can't see him laughing.

Phyllis Diller

Careful! That bunker has a bit of a reputation.

Well if you don't want your meatballs,
just leave them on the side of your plate!

The most advanced medical brains in the universe
have yet to discover a way for a man to relax
himself, and looking at a golf ball is not the cure.

Milton Gross

Years ago we discovered the exact point,
the dead centre of middle age. It occurs when
you are too young to take up golf and too
old to rush up to the net.

Franklin P. Adams

Local rules: A set of regulations that are
ignored only by players on one specific
course rather than by golfers as a whole.

Henry Beard and Roy McKie,
Golfing: A Duffer's Dictionary

I'd rather have him as a partner than an opponent ... That's because he can be pretty sneaky. He'll get out there on the first tee and try to make a match. The first thing he does is talk his opponents out of their handicaps.

Bing Crosby, about Bob Hope

I've always had a wife - golf.
No man should have more than one.

Freddie McCleod

In competition, during gunfire or while bombs are falling, players may take cover without penalty for ceasing play. A player whose stroke is affected by the simultaneous explosion of a bomb may play another ball from the same place. Penalty, one stroke.

Richmond Golf Club, temporary rules, 1940

Just a minute Adam! Where do you think you're sloping off to?

When he gets the ball into a tough place, that's when he's most relaxed. I think it's because he has so much experience at it.

Dov Christopher, Jack Lemmon's caddie

A professional will tell you the amount of flex you need in the shaft of your club. The more the flex, the more strength you will need to break the thing over your knees.

*Stephen Baker, **How to Play Golf in the Low 120s***

I know I'm getting better at golf because I'm hitting fewer spectators.

Gerald Ford

FORE!

Charles never gives any stray balls back...

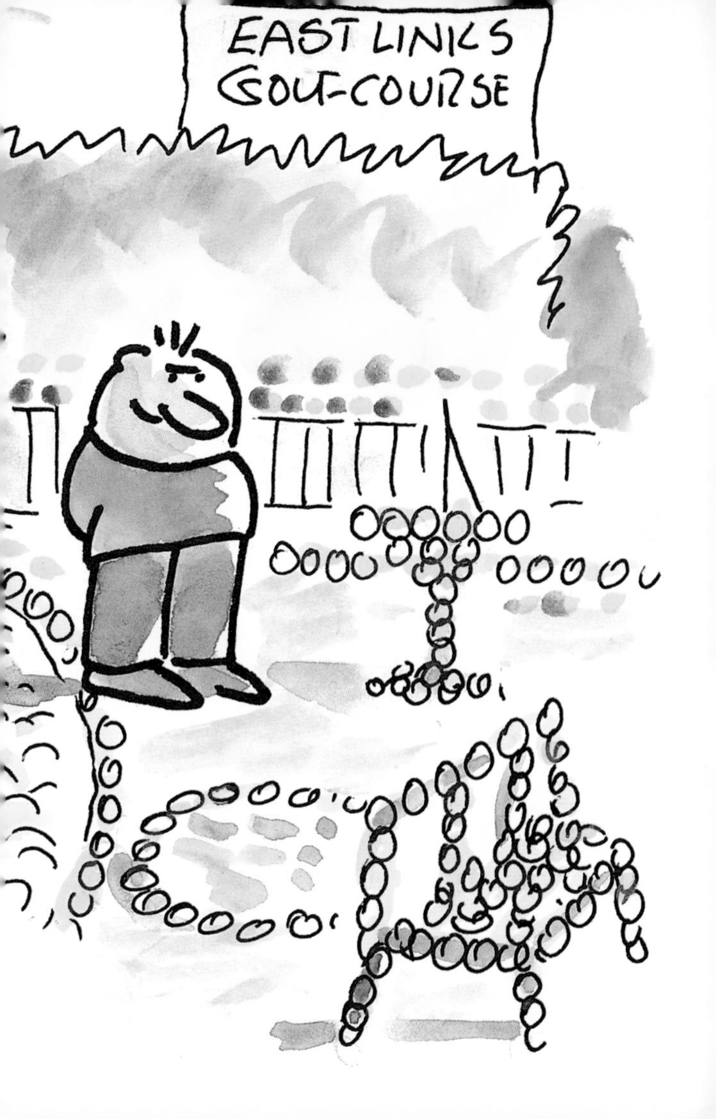
EAST LINKS
GOLF-COURSE

The hardest shot is a mashie at ninety yards from the green, where the ball has to be played against an oak tree, bounces back into a sandtrap, hits a stone, bounces on the green and then rolls into the cup. That shot is so difficult I have only made it once.

Zeppo Marx

He enjoys that perfect peace, that peace beyond all understanding, which comes at its maximum only to the man who has given up golf.

P.G. Wodehouse

A well-adjusted man is one who can play golf as if it were a game.

Anonymous

Golf mad they are round here...

Tragic case – slipped a disc right at the top of his swing...

At least he can't cheat on his score -
because all you have to do is look back
down the fairway and count the wounded.
Bob Hope

A Coarse Golfer is one who has
to shout 'Fore' when he putts.
Michael Green, **The Art of Coarse Golf**

I'd give up golf if I didn't have so many sweaters.
Bob Hope

Golf is a game in which you yell Fore,
shoot six, and write down five.
Paul Harvey, **Golf Digest**

On the seventeenth, beside a main road, the two friends glanced up to see a funeral cortege passing. One of them dropped his club, whipped off his cap and stood with head bowed in reverent silence until the procession was out of sight. Impressed, his pal remarked, 'Good to see old conventions upheld - not many have such good manners, these days.' Replacing his cap, the other man smiled modestly. 'Well we were married for twenty-six years.'

Anonymous

The secret of missing a tree is to aim straight at it.
Michael Green, **The Art of Coarse Golf**

I'd like to see the fairways more narrow.
Then everyone would have to play
from the rough, not just me.
Seve Ballesteros

Good range, dear – but I think the pilot of that jumbo jet will have something to say about his broken window...

I see Wilson's improving his grip...

Aren't you out of that bunker yet?

It's still good sportsmanship to not pick
up lost balls while they are still rolling.

Mark Twain

There are three ways of learning golf:
by study, which is the most wearisome,
by imitation which is the most fallacious,
and by experience, which is the most bitter.

Robert Browning

Playing golf with any President is handy.
If you hit a ball into the rough and it stops
near a tree, the tree becomes a Secret
Service man and moves away.

Bob Hope, **Thanks for the Memory**

There is no need to believe people who say they play golf for the fresh air and the exercise, the ones who tell you they just like to give it a good old bash and never mind who wins, the ones who assure you that they go out in hail, rain and snow just for the fun of it. All these people, every time they stand on the first tee, are expecting to play the round of their life. Pleasure lies in playing well, misery lies in scuffling it into the rough.

Patrick Campbell, **Patrick Campbell's Golfing Book**

I did not want to turn to playing golf, because golf is about as much exercise as shuffling cards.

Bill Cosby, **Time Flies**

For me, it's a game to be played with fresh air in your lungs and joy in your heart.

Peter Alliss, **More Bedside Golf**

Modern course designers don't make things easy these days.

I see Jackson's playing with his boss today...

An *alter kocker* is a man who can no longer do something that he once could ... There are certain activities that are recognizable for old people that only an *alter kocker* gets involved in and golf is one.

Jackie Mason, **How to Talk Jewish**

If you go out with a man who plays golf, your biggest problem will be not to laugh the first time you see him in action. Once they get on the course, the most sober, steadfast and demure individuals suddenly blossom out like court jesters, in the most brilliant colours and fashions - lemon-yellow caps, pale blue anoraks, cherry-pink trousers. And when they wiggle their feet to get their stance right they look exactly like cats preparing to pee.

Jilly Cooper, **Men and Super Men**

Stop moaning – it's cheaper than going all the way to the coast!

Golf is so popular simply because it is the
best game in the world at which to be bad.
*A.A. Milne, **Not that it Matters***

President Ford was playing golf with ice
hockey star Gordie Howe. At the twelfth hole,
Howe conceded a two-foot putt to his distinguished
opponent. Ford insisted on taking the shot - and
missed. 'We won't count that one,' said Howe.
Pointing to the reporters and Secret Service
men at the edge of the green, Ford said,
'Maybe you won't, but they will.'

Most people play a fair game of golf -
if you watch them.
Joey Adams

The same every week –
a couple of gins and he starts playing with his balls...

If there is any larceny in a man,
golf will bring it out.

Paul Gallico

⚐

The City Golf Club in London is unique among
such organizations in not possessing a golf course,
ball, tee, caddy or bag. Its whole premises just
off Fleet Street do not contain a single photograph
of anything that approaches a golfing topic ...

Stephen Pile, **The Least Successful Golf Club**

⚐

I have a tip that can take five strokes off
anyone's golf game. It's called an eraser.

Arnold Palmer

⚐

Golf is a game in which the ball
lies poorly and the players well.

Art Rosenbaum

Particularly pleasing is the story of Queen
Alexandra muddling golf with croquet and, when
on the green, gaily hitting her husband's golf ball
away from the hole and then pushing her own in.

Arthur Marshall, **Sunny Side Up**

Golf and sex are about the only things
you can enjoy without being good at it.

Jimmy Demaret

It took me 17 years to get 3,000 hits. I
did it in one afternoon on the golf course.

Hank Aaron

Sometimes it's difficult for spectators to know
where to stand at all, with any guarantee of safety.

Peter Alliss, **More Bedside Golf**

I got away with it – I told my wife I was visiting relations and the silly fool believed me!

45

Fitness counts for less in golf than in any other game, luck enters into every minute of the contest, and all play is purely incidental to, and conditioned by, gamesmanship.

Stephen Potter, **The Complete Upmanship**

Playing the game I have learned the meaning of humility. It has given me an understanding of the futility of human effort.

Abba Eban

A decision of the courts decided that the game of golf may be played on Sunday, not being a game within the view of the law, but being a form of moral effort.

Stephen Leacock

Income tax has made more liars out
of the American people than golf!
Will Rogers

Baseball reveals character; golf exposes it.
Ernie Banks

No matter what calamities befall him in everyday
life, the true hacker still needs the pressure and
inconvenience of four hours of trudging in wind
or rain or sleet or sun (or all of them at once),
hacking at a white pellet that seems to have a
mind of its own, and a lousy sense of direction.
Tom O'Connor, **One Flew Over the Clubhouse**

I prefer to take out the dog.
Princess Anne, on golf

I was three over: one over a house, one over a patio, and one over a swimming pool.

George Brett

Golf has certainly slowed up at Tuam Golf Club near Galway in the West of Ireland. Players have reported losing a lot of balls – not because of the rough, but because of a large crow. It's carried off dozens of members' balls – on one occasion more than twenty in one day – by snatching them off the course and dropping them out of bounds, and out of reach, in a nearby bog. Among its victims were two golfers on a short hole who'd both made the green in one, and could only watch in fury as the bird swooped down and carried off both balls.

Martyn Lewis, **News at Ten**

The least thing upset him on the links. He missed short putts because of the uproar of the butterflies in the adjoining meadows.

*P.G. Woodhouse, **The Clicking of Cuthbert***

I used to play golf with a guy who cheated so badly that he once had a hole in one and wrote down zero on his scorecard.

Bob Bruce

If God wants to produce the ideal golfer then He should create a being with a set of unequal arms and likewise legs, an elbow-free left arm, knees which hinge sideways and a ribless torso from which emerges, at an angle of 45 degrees, a stretched neck fitted with one colour-blind eye stuck firmly on the left side. And please God, let him be British.

*Chris Plumridge, **Almost Straight Down the Middle***

...And then there was that fabulous 'open' in 1968 where...

I never pray on the golf course. Actually, the Lord answers my prayers everywhere except on the course.
Reverend Billy Graham

Give me a man with big hands, big feet and no brains and I will make a golfer out of him.
Walter Hagen

Bill walked into his place of work wearing a heavy head bandage and knew that he'd have some explaining to do about his accident when confronted by the boss. 'I got it playing golf,' he explained.'My word ... it must have been some size of golf ball that hit you to make that sort of mess!' 'It wasn't a golf ball that did it, it was a club,' he explained further.

'Sit down,' said the boss. 'This sounds interesting.'

Bill sat down gingerly, trying not to make any unnecessary movement with his head and the story began to unfold. 'I was playing a round of golf with my friend,' he went on, 'when my ball veered from the direction I had hit it and ended up in an adjoining field where cows were grazing. When I got there a lady golfer from another group was also busy looking for her lost ball. I found mine without any trouble, then I noticed that one of the cows kept giving a violent twitch of its tail. Lifting the tail I noticed a golf ball stuck in the cleavage beneath the cow's tail. "This looks like yours," I said. It was then that she walloped me with her golf club.'

The Huge Joke Book

A golfer whose ball hits a seagull
shall be said to have scored a birdie.

Frank Muir

If you are ever caught on a golf course during a storm and are afraid of lightning, hold up a 1-iron. Not even God can hit a 1-iron.

Lee Trevino

A member of my husband's golf club raced back to the clubhouse from a lone practice round to announce excitedly, 'I've just had a hole in one on the seventeenth - and I've left the ball in the hole to prove it!'

Mrs K. Plowman

A Coarse Golfer is one who normally goes from tee to green without touching the fairway.

Michael Green, **The Art of Coarse Golf**

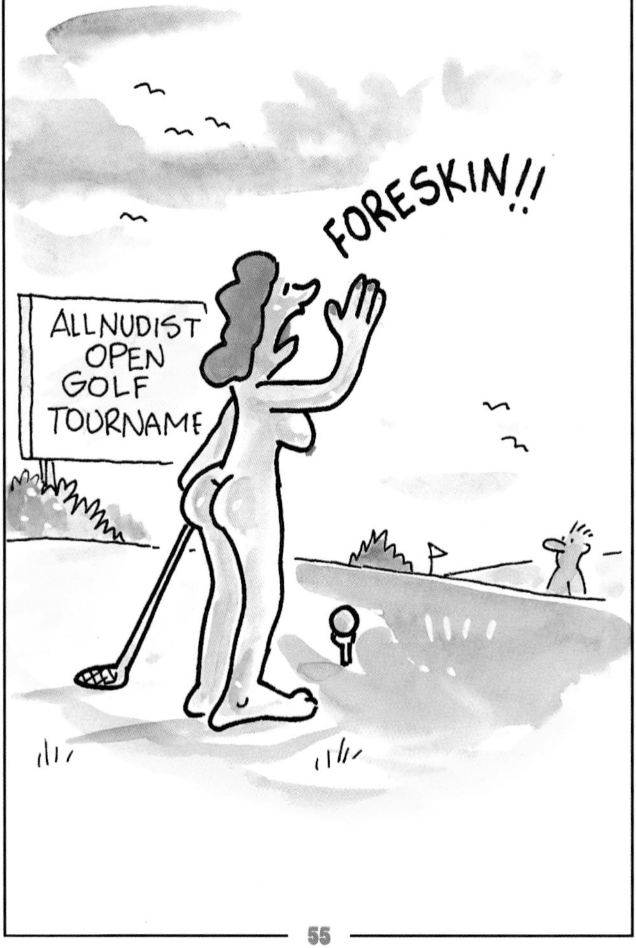
FORESKIN!!
ALLNUDIST
OPEN
GOLF
TOURNAME

Golfer Michael Bonallack, playing in the Amateur Golf Championship at Formby in Lancashire, reached the fourth round by a nose – a spectator's nose. At the fourteenth hole his bunker shot struck the unfortunate observer on the nose, and bounced on to the green instead of ploughing into a nasty piece of rough. As a result, Bonallack halved the hole. He continued to nose ahead – and eventually won by four and three.

Martyn Lewis, **News at Ten**

The uglier a man's legs are, the better he plays golf. It's almost a law.

H.G. Wells

For most players, golf is about as serene as a night in Dracula's castle.

Jim Murray

I wasn't this nervous playing golf when I was drinking. It's the first tournament I've won on the PGA Tour in a sober manner, so it's a great feeling knowing I can do it sober. I don't think two years ago I could have pulled this off.

John Daly

I did warn you he was a bad loser...

A veteran golfer was constantly defeated by the thirteenthth hole. That hole always got the better of him, always made him finish up one or two strokes over par. He told his wife, 'When I die, I want to get my own back on that thirteenth hole if it kills me! Promise me you'll have my ashes scattered all over that damned thirteenth hole.' And sure enough, when he died, after the funeral, his wife solemnly scattered his ashes all over the fairway - and the wind blew them out of bounds.

Bob Monkhouse, **Just Say a Few Words**

Golf is the infallible test. The man who can go into a patch of rough alone, with the knowledge that only God is watching him, and play his ball where it lies, is the man who will serve you faithfully and well.

P.G. Woodhouse, **The Clicking of Cuthbert**

Golfer (very keen to improve his game): 'Do you notice any improvement in me today, caddie?'
Caddie: 'Yes, sir. You've had a haircut.'

Off the dirty little pill
Went rolling down the hill
And rolled right into a bunker.
From there to the green
I took thirteen
And then by God I sunk her.
Traditional

The interesting thing about a Coarse Golfer's language is that to listen to him one would think that his bad shots came as a surprise.
Michael Green, ***The Art of Coarse Golf***

After his last shot, Mr Smith turned to his caddie
and asked: 'What do you think of my game?'
The caddie thought for a moment and then
replied, 'I think your game is quite good, but
I still prefer golf myself.'

A handicapped golfer is one
who plays with his boss.
Anonymous

Golf is the finest game in the
world for making enemies.
*Michael Green, **The Art of Coarse Golf***

I'm playing (golf) like Tarzan
and scoring like Jane.
Chi Chi Rodriguez

Acknowledgements:

The Publishers wish to thank everyone who gave permission to reproduce the quotes in this book. Every effort has been made to contact the copyright holders, but in the event that an oversight has occurred, the publishers would be delighted to rectify any omissions in future editions of this book. *Classic Sports Quotes*, Peter Ball and Phil Shaw, Chancellor Press; *5000 One- and Two-Line Jokes*, Leopold Fechtner, Thorson's; *TAnd Finally ...*, Martyn Lewis, reprinted courtesy of Hutchinson, part of Random House; *The Random House Book of Jokes and Anecdotes*, Joe Claro, reprinted courtesy of Random House Inc.; *Just Say a Few Words*, Bob Monkhouse, reprinted courtesy of Arrow Books, part of Random House UK Ltd; *The Art of Coarse Golf*, Michael Green, reprinted courtesy of Richard Scott Simon Agency; *Time Flies*, Bill Cosby, reprinted courtesy of Bantam Books, a division of Transworld; *More Bedside Golf*, Peter Alliss, reprinted courtesy of Fontana, a division of HarperCollins; *And Finally ...*, Martyn Lewis, reprinted courtesy of Hutchinson; *Almost Straight Down the Middle*, Chris Plumridge, Queen Anne Press.